The Unsinkable

Jackie Sharp

JACKIE SHARP

authorHOUSE®

AuthorHouse™
1663 Liberty Drive
Bloomington, IN 47403
www.authorhouse.com
Phone: 1 (800) 839-8640

Published by AuthorHouse 03/23/2017

ISBN: 978-1-5246-8551-5 (sc)
ISBN: 978-1-5246-8550-8 (e)

Print information available on the last page.

Any people depicted in stock imagery provided by Thinkstock are models, and such images are being used for illustrative purposes only. Certain stock imagery © Thinkstock.

This book is printed on acid-free paper.

Because of the dynamic nature of the Internet, any web addresses or links contained in this book may have changed since publication and may no longer be valid. The views expressed in this work are solely those of the author and do not necessarily reflect the views of the publisher, and the publisher hereby disclaims any responsibility for them.

Dedication

FIRST I WANT TO THANK MY LORD AND SAVIOR FOR GIVING ME THE IDEA TO WRITE A BOOK ABOUT MY LIFE AND HOW HE WAS ALWAYS THERE TO HELP ME.

I WANT TO THANK THE MANY SPECIAL PEOPLE IN MY LIFE WHO ENCOURAGED ME AND HELPED ME THRU MY PERIODS OF PROCRASTINATION. MARIE, MY SPIRITUAL MENTOR, ERIN, MY CLOSE FRIEND OF FORTY YEARS, WHO WE LOST IN 2015, MY SON, TIM, WHO ENCOURAGED ME EVERY STEP OF THE WAY, MY SISTERS IN CHRIST, CONNIE, DIANA, ANNE, SUN, GLORIA AND MY SPIRITUAL FAMILY IN GEORGETOWN, TEXAS, MY HOME HEALTH PROVIDERS PAULETTE, LINDA, PAT, AND NATASHA. AND LAST BUT NOT LEAST, MY BIGGEST CHEERLEADER, THOMAS.

$\mathcal{I}$ am the middle child of seven. I have two brothers and a sister older and two brothers and a sister younger. We were a strict Catholic family who followed all the church rules, like no eating meat on Friday, going to confession on Saturday, and going to church on Sunday and receiving communion. No birth control. I learned about a very punishing God so I was afraid of God, He was too unreachable, so I loved Mary, and baby Jesus.

Daddy was a tall handsome man, who had been a basketball hero in college. That's where he met my mother, a beautiful brunette who made all the front lines in the social who's who. She came from a very wealthy family. Dad worked in Clarks Department Store. I remember sitting in the window of the millinery department watching the parade go by on D- Day .Flags were waving,People were singing and shouting, and throwing confetti out of windows down on the parade. My favorite great Aunt and her sister did the sewing in the millinery department, and they were there with me. I was four at the time. I loved to go to town; I got to pick out my dresses from the racks of beautiful dresses. I never wore homemade dresses, mine were all store bought.

We lived in a big house that had three stories, four fireplaces, and two staircases. It was a beautiful house. My older sister, and I used to play jacks on the vestibule at the front door with one of dads golf balls on the tile floor. The ball would bounce really high, so I would have time to pick up my jacks.

My sister was thirteen months older than me, and then my brother was one year older than my sister. And our eldest was two years older than my older brother. I got teased a lot by my older brothers. We would have tickle contests, but I usually lost.

My little brother was born next. He was four years younger than me. Then my younger sister was eight years younger than me... my older sister and I would help take care of her. She was so cute with her blonde curly hair.

My mother was cold and yelled a lot while I was growing up. Daddy was warm and loving, and I loved him and trusted him. Only he wasn't home very much. He worked long hours, even on the weekend.

We had a housekeeper who looked after us. I loved her very much, but she would not let me kiss her. She was black and back in the forties, blacks didn't have the rights they have today. I never saw color and didn't understand.

My parents were doing pretty well, because we belonged to the country club, ate at high class dinner houses, dressed nicely and had a good life. Mom was gone a lot and our housekeeper spent most of her time with us. My older sister and I played jacks, jump rope and other games most days. Life was pretty good.

Until one Saturday four of us older children were at the movies, as we usually were, when a man sat in the seat next to me. I was five years old. He slowly put his hand up my dress into my panties. I was so scared I froze. Then I got out of my chair and ran home three blocks, ran up stairs to my bedroom, and hid under my bed, until my mother came looking for me for dinner. She never asked what I was doing under my bed... I felt safe there. I use to rock myself to sleep when I was little, and that continued till I was ten or so. I also wet the bed. I would get up in the middle of the night, change my pj's, and get into the other side of the bed, where my sister was sleeping, so I wouldn't get in trouble for wetting the bed. If I got up to go to the bathroom, my brother would jump out and whack me with his pillow and scare me to death.

Living in the city wasn't fun because I couldn't go very far, only to the library, school grounds, or friends in the neighborhood. There were no parks nearby or woods to explore. We couldn't go without shoes, and had to wear dresses most of the time.

A few years later we moved to Washington. Evidently Grandpa and dad had lost their money,so now we were poor........ But it was wonderful! We were allowed to go barefoot, wear shorts and pants instead of dresses, Play outdoors all day after we got our chores done. We no longer had a housekeeper; Mom said we were her housekeepers and babysitters. We had to come right home after school, couldn't belong to any clubs or fun things after school. I lived in books. I went to the library every day and checked out books. I spent hours reading the classics. When I wasn't cleaning house I was reading or playing outside with the neighborhood kids. I loved hiking and playing down by the creek. One time when I did the washing, I put mom's black dress with the white collar in with the dark clothes and faded the collar gray. Mom blew up and told me I did it on purpose and that she hated me and wished I was never born. I was nine or ten at the time.

I was having trouble with my older brother, he became my tormentor. If I told on him things got worse. So I spent a lot of time down the street at my friend's house. She came from a large Catholic family, mostly girls. If I spent the night with her, her father would come get her in the middle of the night. I never understood that, until one day I was alone down in the basement playroom. I had to go to the bathroom, when her father opened the bathroom door and came toward me with his pants down and his penis erect .He grabbed me and forced his penis in my mouth. I bit down, he yelled and I got away, ran home and hid under my bed. I never told anyone and I never went back.

I had cats, lots of them. I used to climb under the grain barn and catch kittens and bring them home. I hid seven cats in my room. I loved them all. Mom allowed me to keep them. I babysat to get the money to buy puss n boots cat food.

I used sand out of my younger brothers sandbox for kitty litter. I was faithful and kept the box clean.

I was an artist and a daydreamer. When my younger brother and my little sister were big enough, we would go to the old cemetery at the end of our street and play in the creek and woods surrounding it. We made Indian teepees out of young beech trees, made a swing with old rope and an oak tree next to t he creek, and swing out over the pond we created by blocking the stream, and jump in on hot summer days. My younger brother made a really cool raft out of tree logs and twine with a barrel on top. We let our younger sister try it out. I'll never forget the look on her face as the raft sank slowly to the bottom of the pond.

There was an old canning company and railroad right behind our house. We would climb on the empty rail cars and ride out to the edge of town, where we would jump off the slow moving train onto a haystack. The hay was for the Shetland ponies they had in the field. We would sneak up on them and try to ride them. In the winter we would go ice skating on the creek that we had Jeannie test to see if it was safe to skate on. She was willing, because she loved to tag along with us.

We lived in a two story farmhouse. The upstairs bathroom was on the other side of the boys room. So I had to go by my brothers bed to get to the bathroom. Our eldest brother was in puberty and had rushing hormones. He was starting to date and wanted to practice sex on me. I was not even starting puberty and knew nothing about sex. I was afraid to refuse him because he had a terrible temper and would threaten me. I threatened to tell mom what he was doing to me. He beheaded my little white kitten. I withdrew into my fantasy world. I could go to a safe place in my mind in order to tolerate the abuse. One day I walked into the garage and he pulled a gun out and held it to my head and pulled the trigger. Of course, it was empty, but it scared me to death. I wanted to escape.

I went to Catholic school and loved the nuns. I wanted to give my life to Christ and be a nun. So when I was fourteen my mother put me on a train to North Dakota to become an aspirant, the first step to becoming a bride of Christ. It was my freshman year. I escaped the sexual abuse, but I was guilt ridden. I even went to confession and confessed my sin. I was given a lecture about it being my fault and a long penitence. I stayed in the nunnery one year. Mother Superior sent me home after that. She said I had living to do before I decided to become a bride of Christ. So I returned home. My older brother had gone into the marines, so he no longer lived at home. Thank God for that.

I was fifteen now and started to become a woman and I was scared to death. I prayed I would not grow up. I even wished Peter Pan was real and would come for me.

I decided I would be a virgin until I fell in love and got married.. I started dating but would not allow any petting or French kissing. The boys called me ice cube.

I had a crush on a boy named Drew. We double dated for awhile, but he dropped me because I would not have sex with him. I was devastated. I wanted to die. That was when I made the first suicide attempt. I walked out in front of an incoming semi-.truck. But someone pulled me back to the curb. My angel, I guess. I didn't realize I suffered from depression, at that time. So I got no help. Little did I know that the Lord was watching over me all my young life. I never learned anything about Him, because we weren't allowed to read the Bible.

I was gifted with talent to draw and paint. .I spent a lot of time drawing. I took art my high school years and painted several paintings. I painted the places I wanted to go to. I had a dream to go to Hawaii. .My sister did too. I spent my junior. and senior years working and saving up enough money so we could go to Hawaii. after I graduated.

I had a really nice boyfriend, Anton, who owned a ski boat . We went water skiing up the Illinois river all summer. I skied upriver 25 miles nonstop to Starved Rock.!

In the winter we would go tobogganing at the park. I was feeling gutsy one afternoon and went off the ski jump on the toboggan and landed on the bar going across the frame with my bottom, and broke my tailbone. I was temporary paralyzed until my friends moved me. Thank the LORD for that. But I didn't. I never saw all the times the Lord was watching over me during my childhood. I felt alone and scared most of the time. I lacked self confidence. I hid my feelings.

In March of 1960, my older sister and I flew to Hawaii. We had worked and saved enough money for the airfare and rent for a month or so. Wow, what a dream come true. I was wide open to all the possibilities in life. I had arrived! I felt bad about leaving Anton, but I was not ready to settle down. I lived most my life in my dream world. I knew nothing about life, real life.

My second older brother was stationed at Pearl Harbor and had found that my older sister and I are in an apartment on the bus route. It was very nice, but the landlady used to stand outside our window and listen to us. My brother and his two friends, Sam and Matthew, also Navy, would buy beer and come over. I didn't like beer very much and really didn't drink. I actually was annoyed by all this since I had a tooth ache. That Monday I saw a dentist and got my tooth taken care of. Then I could enjoy the smell of flowers in the air, and the sound of exotic birds singing in the morning. The whole world opened up in Technicolor. I was in paradise.

My older sister found a job right away, but I was having trouble. I applied at a paint and glass company as a girl Friday. I said I could do anything, just show me how. The boss liked my spunk, and hired me.

Hawaii was beautiful. The beaches were fantastic. My older sister and Matthew, Sam And I, and my other brother and Samantha, a nurse. My brother met there, used to picnic on the beach, snorkel and dive for exotic shells in the crystal clear water at Hanauma Bay. In 1960 there were only a few people on the beach. Needless to say, I fell in love with Sam. He was handsome, tall, dark haired and had deep blue eyes. A country boy from Oklahoma. He told me he had a ranch back in Oklahoma and grew peanuts and cotton.. He said it was his when he got out of the Navy. The idea of Sam in tight fitting jeans, cowboy boots, and a cowboy hat really sounded good. He said he would run horses and cattle. Sounded like a good living to me.

We married on September 3rd, 1960 in a beautiful Catholic Church. My sister and Matthew were our maid of honor and best man. Sam gave me away. We had a small reception, on Waikiki beach. I was happy, I was going to make him happy and love him forever. The morning after our wedding night, Sam threw a quarter on the bed. I was devastated…..He laughed, but my heart was hurting.

My older sister and Matthew married the following month. Later my older brother and Samantha. Life was wonderful! I fainted in the middle of older sister's wedding, and they had to go on without me while I lay down. I was getting nausea in the mornings and finally had to go to the base clinic to see a doctor. I was 3 months pregnant. The baby was due in April of 1961. How was I going to tell my parents. Actually Mom took the news well. In fact the next month my older sister was pregnant and our brother bought Mom a ticket to Hawaii to be with us when we delivered our babies.

Frances was born April 16 in an Hospital in Hawaii. She was only 6 lbs 4oz when she was born. I bonded immediately. I had only gained 13 pounds total so I fit right back into my pants again. I never stopped body surfing, swimming, or mountain climbing in the jungles of Oahu, so I was in good shape.

I was let go from my job when I was 6 months pregnant. My boss felt bad about that so he decided to hire me to work on his catamaran. Sam wouldn't allow it, so I stayed home and took care of him and Frances. Sam was up for discharge and wanted to leave Hawaii and go back to Oklahoma, I wanted to stay in Paradise. My boss invited Sam and I to a party on his boat so Sam could meet Louie, who had come to the islands to build hi-rise hotels. He wanted to hire Sam on, but Sam refused to go to the party. I was devastated. I didn't want to leave Hawaii, I loved it and what an opportunity for Sam.

I left Hawaii with Frances in the late Spring of 61. My watch stopped working at 9am that morning as I was leaving on my flight. It never ran again.

Frances and I arrived in Oklahoma alone and scared. Sam's mom and step dad met us at the airport. We stayed with them six weeks while Sam got his transfer orders and was shipped to San Francisco. He finally joined us at his mom's house. The farm was 140 acre peanut and cotton farm. No cattle or horses. Not at all like Sam had told me. His step dad had no intentions of leaving the farm to Sam. I was so disappointed. I hated Oklahoma. I put everything I had into being a good mother to Frances. She was beautiful. But every day at four in the afternoon she developed colic. I was clueless as to what to do. Thank goodness Sam's mom was there cause she knew what to do. I would turn Frances over to her until Frances fell asleep. Three months after Sam returned I found out I was pregnant again. Sam still didn't have a job. Sam went job hunting when he realized we had to move out of his parent's house.

Being Catholic, I couldn't use birth control. When I went to church on Sunday, I went with the baby. Sam was no help with her.

He finally found work near Duncan, working for the

highway department. We found a garage apt. (upstairs) owned by a lovely elderly couple. We lived there till after Elli was born, eleven months after Frances, on St. Patrick's Day. I named my boy Elli.

We stayed with Sam's parents after I came home from the hospital. Two days after Elli was born, I was in the shower, when I felt a sudden flush of blood into the tub. I was hemorrhaging. I felt faint and the tub was full of blood. I called out for help. Sam came rushing in, grabbed a towel and wrapped it around me, and carried me to bed. He helped me dress in my night gown. The blood was slowing down by then so he just got ready for bed too. I was cold and noticed my heart was racing. I put my fingers on my pulse, my heart was racing and the pulse was very light. Suddenly, the pulse stopped. I lay there wondering if I was dying. Suddenly the room lit up with a bright light and clouds. I noticed I was sitting up, only I was dressed in a white gown to my waist and still connected to my body lying in bed. There was a voice asking me to come with him. I turned and saw a beautiful angel, Elli was his name. He spoke to me but didn't use words. He was beckoning me to come with him. I turned and put my hand thru Sam, who was asleep by then. I thought, I couldn't go, what about my babies. I saw a bright tunnel open before me. I could make out forms in the distant clouds. Elli beckoned to me once more. He said I had a choice to come or not. I looked toward my babies, when suddenly the room was dark again and I was back in my body with my fingers on my pulse, which had returned. The next day Sam took me to the doctor. My blood count was normal. I buried these things in my heart and told no one what had happened. I thought God had given me a chance to leave this world early, but why?

Then we moved to a yard level garage apartment in Duncan. I kept house for the lady and her four children, for the rent. Her house was filthy all the time. I'd clean it up one day and they would have a pig pen for me to clean daily. And I was now pregnant with my third baby.

Sam played baseball in the evenings, when he got home from work. I would have dinner ready for us, then he would leave for the evening, leaving me alone with the children till night. He would come home with bite marks on his arms from wrestling with some girl, or lipstick on his collar, or smell like perfume. I just couldn't believe he would cheat on me, so I would dismiss it. Times were hard, and we were very poor. I finally asked my doctor for birth control pills. I begged my priest to give me permission to use them with no avail.

I was pregnant with my third baby. I was anemic and sick most of my pregnancy. It was hard taking care of babies, fixing meals, doing laundry, cleaning house, grocery shopping on very little budget. The diapers were unending. I had a washer, but had to hang them out to dry. I would freeze dry them in the winter. I got very little sleep.

My neighbor, a Christian dentist and his wife took pity on me and offered us a duplex with two bedrooms for $40 a month. I took in sewing and ironing to earn the money to pay the rent. I asked my neighbors for leftover paint to clean the place up inside. I prayed the Lord would help me provide for my growing family. I went to the Priest to ask for permission to use birth control pills again after Myra was born. I was told it was dangerous for me to have another child. I needed to get built back up again. We could hardly feed the babies we had. I breast fed Myra successfully for eight months, and when she bit me, I put her on a cup.

I fixed beans and cornbread as our staple. I collected pop bottles from the alley to buy bread and milk and peanut butter. I had to take the children with me when I went to the grocery store and I had no car. I had no money for shoes for the children, so I would go to the shoe section and put socks and tennis shoes on my children's feet. I would ask God to forgive me for stealing.

Sam was still running around with his friends after work. I went to my doctor and found out I was pregnant with my forth child. I was 22 years old, living in poverty, and had no hope for a future. I decided I would take in ironing, as well as sewing, to earn enough money to move from Oklahoma to California, where my parents were living .I asked my priest for a hundred dollar loan to help pay for gas to get us there.

Six months later we were headed for California. I had hoped at last......... But I never saw God working in my life. I took all the credit.

California was beautiful! The greenish Blue Mountains, the sweet smelling orange groves, the crystal blue sky was irresistible. I was as close to heaven as possible. We stayed with mom and dad while dad helped Sam find a job. We rented a three bedroom home in North Long Beach. It was darling, and it had a fenced back yard. We went to Sears and bought a houseful of furniture on credit. I was happy with my three babies and Sam and my fourth baby due in December. Sam worked for the tree trimming dept. of Lakewood during the day and he took a second job at a gas station in the evenings during the week, so he was gone a lot. I played with my children and kept house. I would have dinner and a cocktail ready for Sam when he got home at ten pm. The children would be in bed asleep. I was a good wife, mother and housekeeper. I took the children to church with me every Sunday. I was a devout Catholic.

Sam came home early one evening, took a shower, and was getting dressed when he asked me to get him something out of his billfold. I was nine months pregnant, due any day. There in his billfold was a picture of a beautiful girl signed "to Sam with all my love".......I just froze. I asked him who she was and he said she was his girlfriend he had been seeing and he was on his way to her at her mother's house for dinner. He wondered if I would mind if he spent time with her when I was in the hospital having the baby. I didn't know what to say. I just went into a catatonic trance. I couldn't function. I called my mom for help. I don't remember exactly what happened

I was in the hospital trying to deliver my baby, I was having problems. It was two days after Christmas when I delivered Tim. Thank God he was okay. I tried to nurse him, but I was too upset. He was a good baby and took to the bottle right away. My mother had the children while I was in the hospital. My older brother and my sister's husband took a picture of me and the kids over to Sam's girlfriend's house and showed it to her and her mother. They had no idea Sam was married with a family. That ended that. Being Catholic, I didn't believe in divorce, I just buried the pain deep inside and went on as if nothing had happened, except I had to be on medication for depression.

A few years later, we put a down payment on a house in Norwalk. It was a nice three bedroom house with a fenced yard in a nice neighborhood. Lots of young families. I got involved with the ladies in church who also had families. I played with my children. We used to sing songs, finger paint on the driveway, build things with tinker toys and Lincoln logs. I took them to the park and to McDonalds, the new hamburger place. I made all their clothes. Sometimes I would dress them like twins. My children were my life. I would do anything for them.

Sam was working Monday thru Friday at Dairy company as a driver of a delivery truck and earned a decent living, But expenses were going up and we needed more income. We decided I would go to work as a dinner waitress at a neighborhood restaurant. I worked from four to ten pm Friday and Saturday nights. They served cocktails so I had to learn about taking orders of cocktails. We had a uniform we had to wear too. It had a short skirt and fishnet stockings. I made a lot of tips and enjoyed the attention I got. I was worried about the kids with Sam. He had never really taken care of the children and he had to feed them, bathe them, and get them ready for bed.

After a few months of working I noticed cigarettes in my ashtray next to my bed with lipstick on them. Sam said they belonged to the blonde down the street who helped him with the kids when I was working. Up to his old tricks again, I thought. The kids were growing up. Frances was six, Elli was five, Myra was four, and Tim was three. I asked

Frances what was going on. She said Daddy was going in our bedroom and closing the door with the neighbor lady. I asked what she and her brothers and sister were doing and she said playing outdoors.

I confronted him but he denied any hanky panky. I just watched. I figured he was having an affair. I withdrew from him sexually. I didn't know what to do. I had lost my feelings for him. I continued working and saving my money. I started drinking after work and coming home later. I bowled league one day a week and I started drinking cocktails with my girlfriends. I visited my friend, when the three older children were in school. Tim played with her little girl. She said she had a friend I should meet. She introduced me to Joe and Anton. We drank beer, and Joe turned me on to pot. I smoked some and got high. I had never felt that good before. I relaxed and forgot my troubles, and that was the beginning of my crazy life.

I decided I would divorce Sam. I never figured out how I would afford to split up. There was no welfare, food stamps or programs to help me. I would have to get a job and try to make ends meet with what child support I could get from Sam. The courts gave me the house and contents, the kids $7.50 a month per child, child support, and house payment paid by Sam every month.

I found a job at a bushing company for minimum wage. I started at the bottom. They wanted me to learn the business. They made the shells for Remington. Business was booming because of the Vietnam War, I had problems finding sitters. I couldn't afford daycare, and there wasn't much available back then. I was a fast learner, and got promoted after six weeks. But I still didn't make enough money to get decent sitters. I had to start working nights too, to afford child care. My family wasn't any help; they all had their own families and financial problems.

I was short one week and didn't have grocery money. The priest stopped by. I thought he was bringing me a food basket, but he came by to condemn me to hell. He said I was excommunicated because I had divorced my husband. He said Sam had been baptized a Catholic. Sam never set foot in a church or prayed the whole time I was married to him. I was devastated. How could God abandon me and condemn me. I had been a good catholic all my life. I did everything they told me. If He didn't want me, then I didn't want him. That was the biggest mistake of my life!

I worked days at t he bushing company and worked nights at the dinner house until I no longer was able to work for the dinner house. I needed to be home with my children from 5pm till 9pm. So I fixed dinner and got them ready for bed. Then a sitter came from 9pm to 2:30am. I had my sister's friend and her two girls move in for a while to help on groceries. I didn't get much sleep. She turned me on to some uppers so I could stay awake at my day job and downers so I could sleep. I developed terrible headaches. She took me over to some Navy guys house one night to get an aspirin on our way to a dance club. I took the "aspirin" and that's all I remember. I woke up and was naked and it was daylight. I was wet between my legs and could tell I had been raped repeatedly. I found my clothes and put them on. My purse was by the bed, keys and money in it. No one was in the house. I left and went home and showered for hours. I threw her out of my house.

I was so depressed. A year had gone by and I was a mess. My kids didn't deserve this. I called Sam. He said he was leaving California and wasn't going to pay any more child support or house payments. How could I survive. I needed help. My family couldn't baby sit and help me out. My mother and my doctor told me to give the children to Sam to take care of in Oklahoma where he would have his mother and grandmother help with the children while he worked. Just for awhile, while I got well and got some kind of training so I could support the children. I called Sam and presented my problem. I called Sam's mother and told her the problem. She said she could take care of her grandchildren for six months. So I let Sam take my precious children with him to Oklahoma. A week later I got a letter from Frances saying Sam had a wife with him when he took them to Oklahoma. She said she was not very nice. That was the only letter I got from the children. I wrote to them every week and told them I missed them so much and that I loved them. Then I started getting my letters back. With "unable to deliver" no forwarding address on them. Next I got a phone call from their stepmother who told me she told my kids I was dead, And I would never see them again. I was heartbroken. I was on medication and under doctor's care, but I was so depressed that I put my head in the oven, turned the gas on without lighting it, and was going to sleep when my friend Joe came over, found the back door unlocked, and saved me. He stayed with me and helped me get back on my feet again. Then he took me by the hand and led me to the junior college and helped me enroll in classes. I had always wanted to be a registered nurse. So I enrolled in pre-nursing classes. My dream was to become a registered nurse so I could get my children back and support them.

Joe was 21 and I was 27. He was going to college to become a physicist. He was bright but was into drinking, drugs and partying. I started using recreational drugs and alcohol to forget my problems. I fell in love with Joe and eventually we got married. He dropped out of school and joined the Boilermakers union and started working construction. It was good money.

Two weeks after we were married, Joe took me to a college friend's party. I dressed up and we went. I didn't drink much and I didn't use drugs. About 11pm Joe passed out on the couch. I was tired and we couldn't get Joe up. So his friend, whose parents house we were at, told me I could lay down in his sisters bed upstairs and not be disturbed and sleep until Joe woke up. So I went up to bed. I had my clothes on under the covers and the door closed tight. I guess it was about 2am when I woke up with a man in bed with me naked. At first I joked with him about being in the wrong bed, but he would not get out of my bed. He grabbed me and started tearing at my clothes. I screamed but he hit me and told me no one would hear me. I tried fighting him off but he bit me on my neck and held me down and raped me. I screamed, fought, and pleaded for him to leave me alone. I finally got loose and got the door open and screamed for help. She finally came to my rescue. I was crying and telling them what had happened when his sister attacked me calling me a liar and a whore. I couldn't get her off of me. I ran down the stairs woke up Joe, blurted out what had happened and I was calling the police. The guys told me I couldn't do that because Joe brought the dope to the party and he would go to jail. I ran outside and screamed, I wanted to go home, while the crazy sister was still hanging on to me. I grabbed her by her hair and swung her around in a circle a couple of times then let her go. I got in the car and we went home. I never forgave Joe for that. That's when I decided to become permissive. Sex was power, and I was going to be the aggressor.

I was still trying to make contact with my children. I called Sam's mother and she said they moved somewhere in Texas. Wouldn't tell me where. I would write letters to their last known address, and they would come back to me with address unknown.

Then the abuse started. Joe would get drunk and pick a fight with me, and beat me up. First it was a shove, and then it would be a black eye. He would be so remorseful the next day that I would forgive him.

Joe played lead guitar beautifully, He bought me a Yamaha acoustical guitar and taught me how to play rhythm. We played for hours for our friends and partied into the night.

We moved to Torrance so I could attend nursing school there, even with drugs I was getting all A's. I even got on the Dean's list.

Joe started dealing acid. We would drop it on Friday, party all weekend and go back to our normal lives during the week. I got a regular job. I called my wild personality Jackie Sharp Denim.

Joe started partying more with his friends. We even moved in with some of his Harley friends we would ride with. When he was between jobs I would work at the supper club and he would party with his friends. Some of them were really strange. I came home one night, and Joe was high on acid. But I couldn't leave, I loved Joe. So, we would party, play guitar, go camping on weekends and holidays, and he would work out of town and I would take my pre-nursing classes during. the week. Things would be going fine and then he'd get real drunk and beat the crap out of me. One time he broke my nose and put me in the hospital. But I would always go back to him.. That's the viscous cycle of abuse. It was a love-hate relationship. Joe had a stray cat that used to poop on my bed pillow. I hated that cat. I had asked Joe to save the leftover meatloaf for his lunch the next day, but he fed it to the cat instead. So I fixed him a cat food salad sandwich for his lunch the next morning. A week later I stuffed a downer down the cats throat, and behold, the poor cat died.

We moved closer to my college and I concentrated on my studies. I found out I was pregnant when I was a year and a half in my nursing. I was able to go to class up to my ninth month. I was happy I was going to have a baby. I missed my children so much and I didn't know if I would ever get them back.

We had been to the beach the day I went into labor. Joe took me to the hospital, hung around until heavy labor, then left. I was having a difficult time delivering this baby. He was born a blue baby. I had only one placental vein instead of two. They thought He was probably retarded. I was alone when they told me. I cried and I asked God to make him whole. I wasn't able to see or hold my baby boy for 24 hours. In the middle of the night, Joe broke into the hospital, drunk, and fell on me. The police had to escort him out. I felt so alone. I was afraid to reach out to the punishing God I had been brought up with. How could he love a sinner like me?

The next morning they brought my son, Jeff, to me to nurse. They told me he was perfect. Oh, what joy I felt. I would never let this baby get away from me. I would finish nursing school and get a job and earn enough to find my other four children, and take care of my 5 children by myself. I had to stay with Joe just long enough to get through school. He was a binge drinker, so there were times when he was kind and loving to me. He loved having a son. He would play soft rock to him on his guitar and I would play guitar along with him

Then, out of the blue, he would come home from a job drunk and try to pick a fight with me heavy beer glass at me, I ducked and the glass hit the wall above Jeff's crib. Thank God, he wasn't cut by the broken glass. Joe calmed down and went into our bedroom and passed out on the bed.

I called my mom and told her what happened and asked where I could go. She called my brother in Chicago and made arrangements for Jeff and I to go there. I quickly packed up Jeff's and my clothes and caught a red eye to Chicago. It was summer of 1972, and Jeff was just 4 months old.

Chicago was fun. I got a job doing private care nursing, and also working at a nice restaurant for the lunch shift. I made great tips. My friends helped baby sit with Jeff. I made curtains for the apartment to help cover my expenses. We had friends over, played guitars and smoked pot and drank beer. One of them gave me a gift of the use of his car and music lessons at a School of Music. I learned how to play my guitar and got to play along with a few famous people too.

I had a boyfriend named Arthur. He was from a large family like me. He was really sweet not abusive. He was single, young, never married. I was still married to Joe.

In spring of 73 Joe came to Chicago to ask me to come back to California with him. My friends were moving to Colorado and needed to be alone, and I needed to go back to California and finish nursing school. So Jeff and I went back to California with Joe.

It was that summer that I was diagnosed with cervical cancer and had to have a partial hysterectomy. I prayed that I would get my children back, before I died. I ended up with the cancer being stage 2 it had not spread to the surrounding tissue. There again God had rescued me, but I didn't realize it.

I called the school district in Anadarko to see if the kids were enrolled there. Sure enough they were. I got the schools telephone number and called it. I asked to speak to my daughter Frances. The person on the other end said I could not because their step-mother told them only she or their father could call them. I thought about that for a day. Remembering how their step- mother talked, I called again pretending to be her, and asked to talk to my daughter Frances....They said, one moment please, while we get her......hello Frances? This is your mother Jackie; I have been trying to find you for five years. I am not dead, I live in California and I want you to come home. I love you very much…….what is your telephone number and address? I am going to arrange airfare for you and your sister and brothers. Get a pencil and write down my telephone number and address……..I wanted to grab her and hold her and kiss her and tell her how much I have grieved over her and her brothers and sister. I had hope for the first time in five years. I thanked God. I couldn't believe my nightmare was ending.

I called Sam and told him I wanted my children. I was told that he would send the girls, but not the boys. So two weeks later two scared young girls, ages ten and twelve, got off the plane at LAX. And I was in heaven. I was so grateful to have them back. Jeff was 14 months old when they came home. And Joe seemed to enjoy having the girls. So we were one happy family for awhile. I stayed home with the children; cooked and cleaned house made their clothes and played with them. I was so happy. I took them to the doctor. Found out Myra had untreated recurring ear aches that had left her with partial hearing. She said their step-mother would pour salt on cuts. They hadn't had any dental care, and were malnourished .I put them on vitamins and just loved them back to health.

We had to move from that apartment to a duplex owned by my brother, in North Long Beach. Our friend, needed a place to stay so we let him move in too. That was one weird apartment. It had a poltergeist. I would set the temperature off, and the next morning it would be up to 100 degrees. I put duck tape over it and it still would do its own thing.

Also things started disappearing out of the apartment. Odd things like all the shell jewelry, leather belts, and the air gun.

When Frances came home from middle school crying because some girl pulled a knife and put it to her throat in the girl's bathroom, we moved. We rented a large tri-level home in Orange County. Our friend and his five year old daughter also moved in. The house was plenty big enough and we split the rent. I was finishing nursing school, working a private duty nursing job, studying, taking care of four children, and loving it. I drank on the weekends.

Joe got drunk and became violent one afternoon. We were in the van and had the family with us. Joe tried to hit Frances when I got in front of her to protect her; I ended up with a black eye. He escalated so I hit him on the head with a tire iron. That stopped him. So we threw him out of the van and went on. He moved out and I wouldn't let him in to the house again. Our friends helped me. I got drunk and attempted suicide. I ended up in a hospital in intensive care. I remember being out of my body looking down on the doctor and nurses as they were pumping my stomach and trying to revive me. Suddenly it was totally dark and silent…I was scared. I could see a pinhole of light way off in the distance in front of me. I started moving toward it as fast as I could, but it was difficult to move. I kept struggling and moving closer to the pinhole of light. Slowly the hole was getting bigger. when suddenly I popped thru it. I was in a bed and a male nurse said "welcome back"

It was November around Thanksgiving, when Joe came by the house to see his son. I was talking on the telephone when out of the blue Joe thru a heavy ceramic vase at me. It hit the phone at my left ear and tore my ear off. There was blood everywhere and I was passing out. Rhea asked me what happened and I told her before I passed out. I woke up, Joe was gone, but Rhea was standing over me . She got me up and took me to the hospital where they performed plastic surgery on me and sewed my ear back on. They did a great job. I filled out a police report against Joe, but they only kept him over night. I had a terrible Concussion. I was finishing up nursing and facing finals and couldn't focus my eyes. My instructor took pity on me and passed me. I graduated from nursing in December of 1975. It was only by the grace of God that I was able to complete college and become a Registered Nurse so that I could finally support my children.

I couldn't find a job in Los Angeles. There was a strike and no jobs were available. I can't remember clearly but it seems Joe came to see me and ended up hitting me in my face and breaking my nose. I was hospitalized with a severe concussion and had to have my nose fixed. Meanwhile Joe took the kids and all my belongings up to California where he was working for Kerr. He rented a house and moved my kids in. He came to the hospital telling me he loved me and would never hurt me again. I was caught in a vicious cycle. I loved the person who was sober, but couldn't trust him. His father told me I had to quit going back to him, that he would eventually kill me. They didn't have help for battered women back then. So when I got out of the hospital, I went to Trona to get my kids .I ended up staying.

I loved the upper desert. Twenty-five miles east of Trona. It was larger and had a community hospital. The day I applied I had run by to pick up an application for work, but ended up being hired that day as staff nurse on the med-surge wing. I started out at $6.75 an hour. I loved it and excelled at work.

The girls, Frances and Myra, were in middle school and Jeff was in first grade and we're all doing well. I worked 7am to 3pm. So I was home to fix dinner most of the week days. When Joe got off at 4pm, we would go to the Bar and drink and play pool with the contractors from the plant 3-4 times a week. Joe and I bought a three bedroom home in Trona. We got involved in the SBSR, helping rescue people who got drunk and fell into mine shafts. They were all over the desert. The guys would lower me down into the dark shaft first to access the medical situation. I learned how to rock climb, ascend and descend 100 foot cliffs. I had learned to scuba dive back in LA which came in handy if they needed me to cave dive in the lakes up in the mountains.

I got really good on guitar and wrote 21 songs. Joe and I and two other guys formed a band and played at the community center Saturday nights. We were a hit. Every once in awhile we got drunk and ended up fighting. No more broken bones, just bruises. Then he'd go on the wagon and behave himself. I never got introduced to AA or Al-Anon, So I didn't understand why he was the way he was, I was so codependent, and couldn't stand to be by myself without a man. I collected men like notches on a six shooter. I was Jackie Sharp Denim, strong, assertive, in control and unsinkable. When I caught Joe in bed with another woman, I physically beat him up, broke all his china throwing it at him. I was in rage. Then I went home and got drunk. I threw him out but he came back to get me. I put a paralyzing drug in a syringe and brought it home. I thought my only way out was to kill him. I would inject him and the drug would paralyze him for 20 minutes. I would pour a beer down his throat. And he would drown. I was crazy. I had to end the abuse cycle. I got beat up for the last time. I went for help at mental health. They helped me and I divorce him.

He moved out and I couldn't stand being alone. I had the kids, but that didn't fill the empty spot in my gut. He started dating, and I got jealous. I just couldn't let go. I got drunk one night after work, still in my white nurses uniform, and got a gun and went after him. I went to his girlfriends trailer out in the country. No one was there, but the lights were on. I broke the window on the front door with my fist, stuck my hand thru and unlocked the door. I was in rage. No one was there, but I had cut my wrist and was squirting blood all over the place. I wrote in blood on the wall….I'll get you, you son of a bitch." Then I left and went to his apartment. He lived on the second floor of an apartment building with balcony. I climbed up the trellis in my uniform, covered with blood, and carrying a rifle, to the balcony of his apartment. The window was unlocked so I climbed in when someone reached out and took the rifle out of my hands and said "you are one crazy lady" It was his roommate. I burst out crying. He hugged me and told me to go home. I left and went home, fell on my knees in my bedroom, I had no one to turn to but God, and asked Christ to come into my life and help me, I was one crazy lady. Suddenly a warm peace came over me. I felt lifted of my burden. I knelt there and asked God to forgive my sins and come into my life. I was calm and rational. I stopped the bleeding and cleaned up, put my pajamas on, and went to bed I slept like a baby.

When I went to work after that terrible weekend, my friend was talking to me about her church, and invited me to go with her the following Sunday. I said I would. I had trouble really believing God would forgive me completely. But I knew I was saved. My foul language improved and I spent more time at home in the evenings, and out of the bars. I was still addicted to alcohol, but I quit the use of recreational drugs. I didn't have to work at it, it just happened. God was doing for me what I couldn't do for myself.

I got a letter from a judge in Oklahoma saying my son; Elli was being taken from his father's custody and would be given to me if I showed up at the hearing. You know I was there with flying colors. I stayed with Sam. It had been 10 years since we had divorced and I had seen Elli. He was 15 now. He had stolen a car and was joy riding for the second time. I told the judge I was a registered nurse and had a full time position. The judge gave me custody, but I had to come to Oklahoma to court to get him..

I was sexually attracted to Sam and decided to flirt with him and try to get us back together again and be a family. Tim was twelve and didn't want to leave his father. So I took the whole package. I got custody of all five kids. Ten years had passed since I had the boys with me. I was happy. Finally, I got my kids back.

Sam came out to California to look for work at Kerr. He got hired on as a machinery repairman apprentice, and moved in with me and the kids. We went to Los Vegas to get married for the second time. The kids were our witnesses. We were in love and happy. The kids were happy too. Soon Sam was smoking pot and drinking right along with me. We went to the oasis bar and played pool and drank on the weekends. I wasn't as wild as I used to be. I settled down into the role of wife and mother. Just before Myra started high school we bought a house. It had a family room and four bedrooms and three baths. And a swimming pool, which we all loved in the 100 degree plus summers.

I excelled in nursing. I was advancing up in positions. I even got a commendation from the Navy. I was keynote speaker at the local community college nursing program. I was on top of the world.

Sam's dad had left him a Ford 150 pickup truck that we put a cab over camper on and went all over the Sierra Nevada Mountains camping with the kids. We had fun fishing the mountain streams, hiking, and riding the rapids. I took my guitar and played around the campfire. The kids would tell ghost stories and we would roast marsh mellows and make s 'mores. Life was good. We had five wonderful years. Then it ended.

Sam had a silent heart attack. He was put on temporary disability and told to take it easy.

After a year, instead of doing rehab to prepare to go back to work, he decided to continue on disability and retire early. I talked with his MD who said he was becoming a cardiac cripple and was withdrawing from his responsibility. That left me with the responsibility to support the family. He also wanted to sell our home and move back to Oklahoma. I was opposed to that. Elli was married and had a baby on its way. Frances and Jim came back from Kansas and was living with us and helping me. All my children were in California, and I didn't want to leave them. I wanted him to go back to work on light duty and stay in California, where my support system was. Also my job was in Ridgecrest. I should have never have listened to him. I was about to make one of the biggest mistakes of my life.

He insisted and wanted to go back home where it would be cheaper to live. We sold our home, took his retirement and all our savings and moved to Oklahoma. We bought a house in the country on an acre of land outside of Anadarko near his mom's place. I went into deep depression and started drinking heavier. I was on unemployment for the first year' than got a job at the local hospital. Sam joined the country club and played golf everyday with his cousins. .I worked and took care of business while he played every day. He didn't help me with the house work, so I had that to do also. .I resented him and missed my children terribly. I hated Oklahoma, and my life. I felt trapped. Sam had no intention of going back to work. He had retired at my expense.

I changed jobs and got a good job with the State of Oklahoma NTMC program. I was supervisor of Caddo County. .I was off on the weekends. And I drank heavily. I resented Sam and blamed him for my unhappiness. I drank a half gallon of whiskey and a handful of valium and went into a coma for three days; Sam did nothing to save my life. When I awoke, I realized I needed help and admitted myself into a rehab hospital for 30 days. There I was introduced to AA What an awakening. No drugs or alcohol. I had to look at me. I was told to put the plug on the jug and go to ninety meetings in ninety days, get a sponsor and work the steps. I was in a stupor most of the first 30 days, but I did what they said, I really did want to get well. .I felt I really did fit in for the first time in my life. They were telling my story. I finally found understanding; they talked about this thing called a higher power or God. And that I could make him anything I wanted to. I wanted a warm and loving higher power and not a punishing one that would condemn me to hell. He had to be understanding and care about me personally. He had to forgive my sins and accept me just as I was. .And with the help of this higher power I got clean and sober. I got a sponsor and worked the 12 steps of alcoholics anonymous, and found a freedom I had never known before. I was happy, joyous, and free for the first time in my life.

My sponsor had me stay in my marriage the first year of my sobriety. But after that I divorced Sam and sent him on his way. I did not have to put up with his verbal abusiveness any more. Jeff was 15 at that time and Sam had been tremendously abusive to him. I was sick and tired of marrying abusive men, I wanted to find a nice guy to settle down with. O f course I still had that hole in my gut that I had to stuff a man in, because I couldn't be alone, I *was terribly codependent* .So I dated several guys in AA, none of which fit the bill.

Then came Julius, a jolly little fat man who seemed happy joyous and free with 20 years of sobriety. Everyone looked up to him and he swept me off my feet. So I married him. By this time Jeff had moved out of the house and in with his best friend and sued me for child support. I couldn't stand living by myself, so I said yes to Julius. I knew nothing about him, except that he was divorced, had two kids that had nothing to do with him, had no credit and owned nothing. I had excellent credit, owned a house paid for, and a new car, and had a great job. After three years, bankruptcy, no money in the bank I divorced him and realized he was a con artist. I was devastated and had a nervous breakdown.

My friend May from AA moved in with me. No more men. I had severe depression and suffered from anxiety attacks and had to go on medication. Julius started stalking me and scaring me. I finally was unable to work. Employee assistance at work found a hospital in Arkansas that would take me. I was admitted with post traumatic stress for 30 days.

It was intense work, that covered my childhood sexual abuse up to the present abuse. I learned a lot about the abuse cycle, co-dependency, anger and depression.

May befriended me and helped me during that time .I trusted her. She had use of my home and my car while I was gone. My family wasn't in my life, they all lived so far away, and so May was all I had.

I was better when I got home, but I was on medication for depression and anxiety. I had noticed May had started taking over and she was having mood swings. I shrugged it off and continued to let her stay at my house. I was shunned by my AA so called friends because I was on what they called "mind altering drugs". My sponsor quit and told me I was not sober. I had seven years of sobriety! I was devastated.

May suggest we sell the house and move to Colorado. I agreed to that. I wasn't welcome in Norman anymore. Julius was still stalking and had told vicious lies about me. May was my only friend, so I sold the house. She wanted to go to a town northwest of us and stay with her old boyfriend until spring. I was not capable of making rational decisions, due to the medication and stress I was under. So I agreed.

May started saying I was doing bazaar things. Like sleepwalking and pulling knives on her. She took me to a Psychiatrist friend of hers. She admitted me into a psychiatric hospital. They increased my meds and kept me for 30 days. May was taking care of my business, talking to my family, and friends. She convinced them I was being taken care of well. She had me ask my brothers for money to cover expenses. The doctor suggested I give May Power of Attorney so she could take care of all my business and get me on disability. His wife helped me sign the papers, since I was too drugged to do it myself.

I lost control of my bladder and had to wear adult diapers. I drooled, and could not dial a phone. I had no idea what was happening to me.

May would bring me home on weekends, and terrorize me and over dose me. I was a prisoner. Finally she sent me to a state mental institution. I was admitted by the court for the criminally insane. I was in a lock up ward and unable to care for myself. They said I had tried to kill May and her boyfriend with a knife in the middle of the night. No one listened to me. I knew I hadn't done anything.

It was cold and I couldn't get warm. They made me strip and take cold showers in the morning with no soap, shower curtain or heat. I had most of my nice clothing stolen from me, so I wore old sweats nobody wanted. I don't remember much during that year and a half. I found the only friend I had was Jesus. I could remember some scripture. I walked and talked with Him daily. He took away my fear and gave me hope. I knew He would rescue me someday. No one called or visited me. It was as if I had disappeared from this earth.

A few months later, May moved me to a nursing home. I had no idea where I was. May would take me to her boyfriend's house on weekends. She was mean and scared me. I was so drugged I had no defense. She overdosed me on my meds the nurses had sent home with her.

I liked the nurses and the nursing home. They were kind to me. I would go out on the patio and garden and pray and talk to my Lord. I had nothing, was nothing and turned my life and will over to the Lord. He gave me great comfort. Also I knew he would rescue me.

My friend Erin had been trying to find me for months. May wouldn't give her any information about where I was. May had told her I was in the nursing home because I had Alzheimer's disease and couldn't have any phone calls. Finally, Erin tricked May into giving an address. Erin called the nursing home and talked to the nurses. She found out May was posing as my sister and power of attorney, and had told them all kinds of bazaar stories about me. Erin contacted Adult Protective Services, who immediately sent a worker out to see me. The worker was a nurse I had worked with two years earlier. So she knew me .She asked if I was scared of May, of course I said yes. I was so doped it was hard to get much out of me.

All of the sudden my sister and her husband appeared at the nursing home. They said they had a vision from the Lord to come to Oklahoma and rescue me. My dear sweet Jesus had sent a rescue squad. My sister took care of all the legal proceedings to get power of attorney away from May and to protect me from her.

Erin arrived January 12. 1995 with a U-Haul truck to pack me up and take me home with her in New York. About that time my son Elli showed up to help rescue me and pack up all my belongings. Jeanie, Erin and Elli wanted to go to May's house to pack up all my household belongings. Everything I owned had been stolen by them. May refused and then brought some of my personal belongings to the nursing home. She kept all my furniture and appliances. Evidently May had stolen all my savings and disability and insurance checks. All together she had stolen $25,000.00 from me and run up all my credit cards. She had my Mustang repossessed. And taken two years of my life. The District Attorney and the police could do nothing. I would have to sue her in civil court and prove ownership of my houseful of possessions. I had no money and was scared to death of her. Jeanie found out that she had bought a burial plot for me. I was lucky to get away with my life. I had lost everything, but had gained a freedom I had never known before. My Lord and Savior had saved me and given me a new life.

Erin and I had perfect weather to drive to Wilson, New York considering it was January. We stopped in Youngstown, Ohio at my son Tim's house on the way. Dan instructed Erin how to wean me off of all the drugs I had been on. I was in pretty bad shape.

I don't remember much about the first year at Erin's except she loved me back to health and off all those psychotropic drugs. She took me to a little Baptist church on Sundays. I had so much to be grateful for. I was a totally different person. I had a relationship with the Lord no one could ever take from me. I had everything, although I owned nothing.

I no longer had that hole in my gut. The need for a man was gone. If God wanted me to have a mate, He would have to give him to me. My picker was broken.

I stayed another year with Erin and her family. I was getting stronger every day. She and I had a lot of fun together. We even started a fused glass business together. Stick-lizard Glassworks was a success. We made beautiful jewelry, sun-catchers, slumped bowels, snowflakes, and whatever else we could create. It kept me busy and useful. We had a Christmas Holiday sale in December at her house. Erin worked days at a power plant job and I held down the fort at home.

It was late December, 1995, when I met Tom. He came by the house to find a gift for his mother. I was baking Christmas cookies. I noticed him and thought he was really nice and left it at that.

A week later Erin told me she wanted me to go to her friend Candy's Christmas party. She had to work swing shift and was unable to go. I didn't really feel like going to a party, but I decided I would go anyway. When I knocked on Candy's door, Arthur answered it. He acted really happy I was there. We immediately became friends. I met his mother and saw most of Erin's neighbors there. When I left, Arthur invited me to a New Year party the following week. I accepted. People seemed to be happy to see us together. Arthur was single and never married. He just celebrated his 50th birthday. He was a good Christian and invited me to attend church with him. I thanked God for sending me a friend.

Erin had taken me to her doctor for medical care. I was finally off the drugs I had been on. I did remain on a mild antidepressant and blood pressure pills. Erin enrolled me in the YMCA water exercise program twice a week for some contractures I had developed from being incarcerated. She also had me walk daily down to her neighbor Susie's house for coffee. Everyone was wonderful to me and had babysat with me at one time or another. Wilson was a small town so everyone knew about me.

In1997 I decided to move out on my own in an apartment 15 miles north of Erin. I applied for Samefits and got in a 1 bedroom upstairs apartment. That was the first time I ever lived by myself. But I wasn't alone, God was there.

Tim and family lived four hours south in Ohio. Erin would drive me half way down and Ashley would pick me up half way up at least one weekend a month. I was so grateful to have my grandchildren in my life. We would play games all day. Life was wonderful.

My daughter Myra lived in Maryland with her husband and two children. They were precious blonde curly haired with unlimited energy. I would go out for drinks and dinner with Myra while Brian would baby-sit. It didn't take long to realize I was back to my old habits. I was drinking the hard stuff. And I was smoking 1-2 packs of cigarettes a day.

I was out to a bar with Myra and a couple of girlfriends, when I suddenly couldn't breathe. It scared me so bad that I decided to quit smoking that was May of 1999.

I had a couple of episodes that took me to the hospital. I was diagnosed with COPD. I had moderate emphysema.

I started praying for help to stop drinking. I was trying to live a good Christian life without alcohol. I decided to just drink wine occasionally. That worked for awhile. I joined Tom's church and became active in it. I loved the ladies and the Priest. I went to Bible study every Thursday after services; I was absorbing as much from the Bible as I could. I started reading it every morning and praying for my family and help to be a better Christian.

Arthur and my relationship were becoming stronger. We went to church every Sunday together and helped his aging mother. She and I became very close. Arthur and I liked to go to the Finger lakes to the wineries. I was learning all about wines and what wine went with what meal. We enjoyed having a glass or two with our meals. He would bring me a bouquet of flowers every payday. It wasn't long and I fell in love with him. I just knew he was the one God had sent for me. He proposed to me at Niagara Falls, even got down on one knee. It was so romantic. The ring was beautiful. A heart shaped stone.

We moved Arthur's mother up to an apartment under my apartment in Sanborn so I could help her and prepare meals for her while Arthur was at work. She was getting more frail and forgetful. I grew to love her dearly, although I would become very frustrated.

Arthur had changed jobs and was working for Bank of America. He was doing very well in the financial world, so we set the date of our wedding for February 15, 2003. I was so happy. I planned our wedding with the help of our church friends. And we were married at St. John's on the coldest day in February. We spent our honeymoon in Niagara Falls. It was one of the happiest days of my life.

We planned a trip out to California to visit my daughters. I was so excited. I hadn't seen my daughters for a couple of years. Myra had moved to California, divorced and bought a house near Frances. The morning we were getting ready to catch the plane to California, Arthur broke down and said he couldn't go. He was crying and was having a panic attack. I tried to calm him down and get him to go, but he wouldn't. I had to cancel our trip and reservations on a non refundable ticket. I called mental health where I was being seen. He started therapy for depression and anxiety. I was devastated. He seemed so normal. I hadn't seen this coming. We just got married two months ago and he was fine.

He went on a leave of absence from work. That lasted two years. He was hard to live with during that time. He would get angry and upset me. I was having doubts about marrying him. Was he abusive too? All my dreams for us were shattered. I continued my church and Bible studies. I wanted to learn more. I wasn't learning anything in our Bible study at church. They spent the time talking about other things. I read a daily devotional and the Bible daily. But I started drinking wine on a daily basis. Then I got the devastating telephone call...Elli had killed himself! My baby, my sweet gentle Elli was dead. He left a wife and four children behind. That was a hard year. I drank to not feel the pain. I was diagnosed with breast cancer and had a lumpectomy and radiation treatments, and Arthur's mother died. A year later, my mother died. Only the Lord carried me through.

The next year I had my first knee replacement, followed by my second. I had terrible arthritis and it was unbearable in the icy cold winter of Western New York.

My son Tim in Texas wanted me to move down to Texas to be near him and my grandchildren. He said he would buy me a house. I had visited him there several times a year. I loved East Texas. The weather was so much warmer in the winter. I had arthritis and suffered from pain and stiffness really bad all winter in New York which lasted six months out of the year. I told Arthur about the opportunity to have a house and my desire to be near my children. He would not hear of it. He hated the south and would not ever move away from his friends, who were all women by the way.

I had been going to church with Tim and the family every time I visited. I met Kim in Sunday school, she was the teacher. We clicked like two peas in a pod. We instantly became good friends. I learned so much about the word of

God from her and at Central Baptist Church. I was being drawn there.

I prayed about the move to Texas, and in May of 2006 Tim and Ashley, and my grandson came up to move me to Texas. I left Arthur behind. He had chosen to quit his job with a future and great Same fits and go on disability and work odd jobs. He stayed in western New York. I figured he would follow me down to Texas later.

Tim got me a nice three bedroom, two bath brick home in an older neighborhood. It was only 5 blocks from Marie's house. I loved it. I had a miniature black poodle named Gypsy who moved with me.

Arthur came down to visit me in October, when it was cooler weather. He stayed a couple months, decided he didn't like it here and wouldn't stay with me. The hot weather was too hard on Gypsy so I let Tom take her with him back to New York. Also Arthur missed her more than me.

I started buying boxed wine once a week. I would have a couple of glasses in the evening before supper. I checked out the dog rescue sites on my computer looking for a small white companion dog. I fell in love with a 9 year old Maltese. I called the phone number and found they still had the dog at a temporary home near Dallas. Kim went with me to pick her up. Her name was Crystal and she was adorable. I fell in love with her instantly. Tim had the back yard fenced for me so Crystal could run and play out back.

Arthur would visit in the spring and fall. Finally I told him we didn't have a marriage, I wanted all of him or nothing. That was in 2008. He left and didn't come back. He wanted to remain friends though. I fell into depression. I went to mental health and got back on antidepressants.

I challenged the Texas nursing board and got licensed as a RN in Texas. I got my first job in 14 years. I started working as RN supervisor on weekends at a nursing home in Rusk, 15 miles south of my house. I worked there three years. I was doing great until I noticed I couldn't run up and down the halls without getting short of breath. My legs ached and I couldn't stand for very long. I had to quit working the floor and only do supervisor work. I had started drawing social security in 2006, so that and my earned income made it possible to pay the bills. I had used most of my savings to buy a 1 year old used car. So I had to work. I started buying two cartons of wine a week.

During the week I went to ceramics, Bible study, played cards, and worked out at the gym. I had started to gain weight. The doctor put me on steroids for my lungs and that made me eat more. I was put on oxygen at night. I prayed that God would heal my lungs. I needed to work to live.

I had joined my church and was baptized soon after I got to Texas. I also asked to be saved again. So why couldn't I stop drinking. I hid it from my family and friends only drinking after five pm and never leaving the house after starting. Only Erin knew. She also moved to Texas in the fall of 2006.

In 2009 I changed jobs and went to work for a nursing home here in town. It was a lot nicer work environment and much more enjoyable. The work was pretty easy, so I didn't have the problems I had before.

I started having memory problems, and got confused easily. I was forgetting to tell my supervisor important details. I also noticed I couldn't go very fast down the halls, and I would get light headed and short of breath. I went back to the doctor and he did some tests. He said I had severe COPD emphysema and moderate dementia Alzheimer's and put me on more meds. I had to quit my job in December of 2010. It broke my heart.

Now I had to live on $1200.00 less a month. My bills exceeded my income. I became more depressed and I started drinking hard liquor instead of wine daily. My health was getting worse and I was put on oxygen 24/7. By March of 2011, I was drinking a gallon of whiskey a week. My dear friend, Virginia, died and Arthur called to tell me Gypsy had died. I was grieving and in a deep depression. I had held on to the idea that Tom would get back together with me all this time when my friend Erin told me Arthur said he would never get back with me. He was happy without me.

Times were tough financially. Tim wanted me to rent out my spare bedroom for $400 a month and keep $200 and give him $200 so he could meet his expenses on the house. I panicked. I was afraid to let a stranger in my house because of what had happened with May. I had quit taking my medications and had slipped into depression. I was becoming suicidal and felt hopeless. I got up one morning, started drinking heavily. I was crying and calling my girls and Arthur. I went into a blackout and called 911 for help. I didn't want to kill myself but felt no way out. Soon the police came and took me to the hospital. My blood alcohol was 1.8. I don't remember much, but later that night they transferred me to Behavioral Health center for admission. *I didn't realize it, but God was answering a prayer I had prayed for a long time. I had wanted to quit drinking and get sober and He had placed me in a position to do so. The next morning the nurses took me to an AA meeting. I felt right at home. God had given me a way to get sober and learn to live life on life's terms. I was filled with fear and was trying to do it myself. I wasn't relying on God. AA gave me a program to follow that would lead me to depend on God. I was in the treatment center for five days. The doctor put me on different meds and the depression lifted. I went home and went to an AA meeting where I got a happy sponsor and who immediately had me work the steps. I did a though forth step followed by fifth,six and seventh steps. I was relieved of the desire to drink and my fears were falling away. I prayed every morning and night asking God to keep me sober and to make me useful to others. I became much closer to my God. I was happy, joyous, and free!*

I started volunteering at church and working with others. My spiritual mentor, Kim, helped me grow by leaps and bounds. My past was becoming my greatest asset. I was helping other women who had gone thru what I had, find the Lord too .God had given me a purpose that mattered.

I live alone with my beloved Crystal in a small one bedroom apartment. I no longer worry the next meal will come from or how I will pay my bills. God provides my every need. I have lived without a man for seven years now. I have let go of Arthur and am good friends with him now. We phone each other several times a week. Sam and his wife moved down here and we get together with the kids and grandkids on the holidays. I am at peace at last.

September 1, 2013, I received devastating news. My beloved daughter Myra had hung herself and was dead. My twenty-one year old granddaughter found her. How do you survive something as terrible as this? I asked my sweet Jesus to help me, and he sent me peace, Knowing Myra had been saved and that she was ill with depression and alcoholism, I knew she was in heaven with Elli and Mother, and at peace at last.

I was able to fly to California with the family, even though I had oxygen 24/7 and could walk only short distances with a walker. The airline was a wonderful help, as well as my granddaughter who is a RN, and my son, Tim, who is a M.D. and two grandsons. We gathered the family at Frances's in Ridgecrest, California and had a beautiful memorial service. God held me together and held the family close thru the week. I was in shock.

I grieved for over three years the loss of my two children. During that time my health worsened and I had to move out of my apartment into an assisted living home, twenty five miles from my friends and family. I was hospitalized five times that year with pneumonia and congestive heart failure. Why I'm alive I don't know except to help other women and finish this book.

I was rescued from that assisted living home by my daughter-in-law, Ashley and her husband Elli, who moved me to her mother-in-law apartment at her house in Georgetown, Texas in November of 2015, where I reside today. I have my granddaughters and my grandsons and my darling great grand babies in my life. I watch the deer every morning and every evening in the field out back crossing thru the yard.

I am home now, but knowing my dear sweet Jesus is taking care of my Myra and Elli. Life goes on and I know we can still have peace and joy in our lives, no matter what happens.

Philippians 4:6-7 Don't worry about anything; instead pray about everything. Tell God what you need and thank Him for all He has done. Then you will experience God's peace, which exceeds anything we can understand. His peace will guard your hearts and minds as you live in Christ Jesus. Amen!

Epilogue

I believe I was being led to write this book in order to help others who have walked down this road too. Hopefully it will give them the courage to reach out for help and surrender their old way of life for one of peace and joy.

Printed in the United States
By Bookmasters